# MY FIRST EARTH DAY

# MY FIRST EARTH DAY

## Karen Katz

**GODWINBOOKS**

Henry Holt and Company
New York

Henry Holt and Company, *Publishers since 1866*
Henry Holt® is a registered trademark of Macmillan Publishing Group, LLC
120 Broadway, New York, NY 10271 • mackids.com

Copyright © 2024 by Karen Katz.

Our books may be purchased in bulk for promotional, educational,
or business use. Please contact your local bookseller or the Macmillan Corporate
and Premium Sales Department at (800) 221-7945 ext. 5442 or by email at
MacmillanSpecialMarkets@macmillan.com.

Library of Congress Control Number: 2023937876

First edition, 2024
Book design by Gene Vosough
The art for this book was created with gouache, colored pencils, and collage.
Printed in China by RR Donnelley Asia Printing Solutions Ltd., Dongguan City,
Guangdong Province

ISBN 978-0-8050-7895-4

For Gary, who loved this earth

Today I am going to celebrate Earth Day with Nana. She knows all about taking care of our planet.

Nana and I have cloth bags to carry everything we will need.

We take seeds for the garden, tiny trees to plant, water in our special bottles, and some sandwiches.

We won't forget our sun hats!

We go to Nana's vegetable garden.

BELL PEPPER

TOMATO

LETTUCE

Nana says growing her own vegetables saves her trips
to the supermarket and helps keep our earth healthy.
We plant some beans. I will watch them grow all summer.

SEEDS

BEANS

CARROT

RADISH

We walk to the edge of the forest, where we plant our little trees.

I plant an elm tree and Nana plants a fir tree.

She says we must keep the trees growing or terrible things could happen.

The air would get dirtier, there would be more mudslides, and animals would lose their homes.

"Let's go look in the forest," says Nana.

I see birds, deer, squirrels, raccoons, and bunnies.
So many animals make this forest their home.
What if they didn't have a place to live?

On we walk to the lake.

The water is sparkly like jewels.

"Our water is very precious," says Nana.

Nana reminds me that if we use too much
water or don't keep it clean, we could run out
and have nothing left to drink.

I think about our beautiful oceans, lakes, and waterfalls.

We need to care for them.

What would happen to the fish and sharks and octopuses?

"Let's take the bus into town."
I see so many cars on the road.
"All those cars putting out
exhaust makes our air dirty,"
says Nana.
"What if more people took the
bus like us?" I ask.
"Good idea, little one!"

We arrive at the farmers market. People come from nearby to sell their products.

"Look at all the fresh fruits and beautiful flowers!"

Nana loves to support the local businesses.

We buy some strawberries to take home.

"I'm hungry, Nana. Let's eat!"

"Look, Nana, there is trash everywhere!"

"Let's pick up what people left behind,"
she says.

We find candy wrappers, paper cups,
plastic bottles, and even a diaper.

We recycle the paper and plastic, and
we throw away the trash.

Keeping the earth clean is fun!

"Come, little one. It's time to go home."

We stop to watch the sunset on the way home.

The sun is so warm.

Nana tells me the earth is getting hotter because we haven't been taking care of it.

She says ice is melting in the north, and polar bears and seals have nowhere to go.

I imagine all the animals that live in the cold Arctic. Where would they go?

At last we get back to Nana's house.
   I think about the forests, the water, all
the animals, the fish, and the sun.
   I think about all the ways I can take
care of our earth.

I have an idea . . .

Look, Nana!

How to help the earth!

take the bus

plant a tree

use a cloth bag

turn off the lights

I made a picture just for you!

Thank you, Earth.